HOW DOES YOUR GARDEN GROW?

Written by

Ann J. Clarkson

Illustrated by

Marilyn Church

To Ava,
I know your
garden will be
rich and beautiful!
Ann

How Does Your Garden Grow?

A View of Making a Garden and Building a Life

ANN J. CLARKSON, Author

To Lorelei, Will, and Gracelyn,
Lovely new sprouts in my family's garden.

MARILYN CHURCH, Illustrator

To my Grandsons, Jackson, Ben, and Sam

Just being outside has often been a relief from worry, a prelude to a new perspective, or a rest from the increasingly conceptual and technological activities of everyday life.

Recently, as I worked outside, I began to realize that so much of the thought process that goes into gardening and landscaping, perfectly applies to building a life.

And so, as one generation has done since the beginning of communal life, I wanted to pass on to younger generations some of the ideas I have come to believe.

What better way than a book?

Have a Plan for Your Garden

As time goes by, your plan can change (and probably will) but you will have a place to start, some ideas to explore, and lots of interesting things to learn.

Just focusing on an idea will open up exciting things to think about.

And some of those new things you learn may lead you down paths you never knew were there.

Sometimes it pays to seek advice from an expert.

It is true that people can focus their time,
energy and intelligence to know a lot about one subject.

That person can become an expert.

Sometimes an expert can give you information that can answer questions for you,

give percentages that may help you favor one course over another,

or share their own experiences.

The advice the expert gives you **may help you avoid** expensive or time-consuming
activities that don't pay off in saved time and money.

BUT...

…Sometimes it pays to ignore the experts.

You see, those experts probably have never been in *your* garden,

or talked to you about the vision in your head.

They don't know your capacity to think, work, and plan.

In short, consider advice and new information,

but in the end, *it is your garden.*

Sometimes you have to use common sense.

I don't care how much you love orchids...

If you live in Alaska you won't have them outside in your garden.

The circumstances of your garden in many cases are predetermined.

But the details within those circumstances are endless!

Just look around any neighborhood.

The climate, soil, rainfall and amount of sun are the same.

But, the differences in the way people use them are amazing.

That is where your creativity comes in, where you can use your ability to think carefully, and your willingness to

PLAN YOUR WORK

AND

WORK YOUR PLAN.

Different plants

have

different needs.

Sunflowers and impatiens
are both beautiful.

But they have far
different needs.
One needs a lot of sun,
while the other needs
a lot of shade.

Is one better than the other?
Is one more beautiful?
Or is one more desirable?

You can see the answers to
those questions are an opinion,
not a fact

But there is one
FACT
that you must
consider.

The needs of these plants are
very different.

If I love sunflowers, and do
the necessary work,
then there is **no** reason
I should not have
fields of sunflowers.

Or I can have rose gardens,
or beds of impatiens.

But it would be very hard to
have them all in one small
flowerbed.

You're going to need tools.

Even the tiniest garden space, worked by the most diligent gardener, needs tools to help.

Sometimes the tool needed is simple and easy to find.

Sometimes the job to be done is larger and takes more effort to decide what tool to use.

To solve any problem, use the simplest approach first.

I would say that a gardener's success stems a lot from their willingness to learn and to use a simple tool first.

Then move on to more complicated solutions to fit more complicated problems.

Taking care of a garden is hard work.

There are rocks that have to be dug out and moved.

There will be lots of weeds that need to be pulled.

You will have aches and pains, scratches and bruises.

However, in the end you have spent your energy on something worthwhile and lasting.

Now *that* kind of project is worth it!

Don't always plan for an easier garden.

Remember, if it is easy, lots of people will do it.

Easy jobs always have lots of competition.

Want to be sought after?

Look for a harder job, and learn to do it well.

Build a more interesting garden.

When you run into a wall, step back.

That seems pretty obvious, doesn't it?

But you would be surprised how many people

keep banging into a wall, expecting it to move.

It almost never does.

Taking a step back will help you see that wall in another light.

Maybe you can use that wall to become a building block in your garden.

It might even become a beautiful part of your plan.

Don't skip the basics.

You can spend a lot of time in a garden,

but if you don't tend the basic ingredients needed

(in this case, soil) you will waste a lot of time.

You see, this kind of work does not get a lot of praise.

You will be on your knees, in your dirty clothes, repeating a task many, many times.

You are building a foundation and it is not done quickly.

Another basic idea in a garden is balance. Japanese gardens are built around a concept that includes water, rock, plants and living creatures, all in harmony.

There are things that were in your garden first.

Make friends with them.

You don't love worms?

Are you afraid of bugs?

Does it help to remember they have a job to do in the garden?

In fact, worms make garden soil healthy.

If those worms and bugs had not been working for many years before you got there, you could never grow anything.

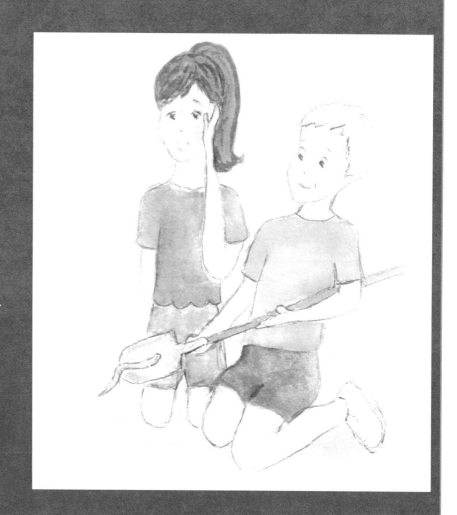

Every garden will have weeds.

Pay attention to the weeds.

What, exactly, is a weed, and how do you plan to deal with them?

Some people say that anything in the wrong place is a weed.
Others say a weed is any plant they just don't like.

Weeds grow very fast, and they have a very shallow root system.

Many of them do damage to the plants you might want in your garden.

Certainly, weeds take up space
that could be put to better use.

No matter how you choose to name a plant a weed,
if you really don't want it in your garden
and if you decide that your garden will be better off without it,
the earlier you remove it,
the easier it will be to remove it completely.

Does it work to plan to rake leaves in the spring?

There are right times and wrong times to do special work.

Things work better if you take advantage of the rhythms of life.

Once you have prepared the soil, take the next step.

Wait a bit to see how things develop.

Then go on with the next step,
and the next,
until you see the plan taking shape.

Don't try to dig weeds in the driving rain.

Don't kid yourself.

You will make mistakes.

Mistakes are nature's way of making you stop

and take another look.

The only people who never make mistakes are

people who never do anything.

You don't want to be one of them, do you?

Please remember that every garden is,
and should be, different.

It is okay to get a few ideas from a neighbor's garden,
but just because you think that garden is beautiful,
does not mean that it would fit into your plan.

Be willing to help, if asked, when friends need help in their gardens.

Be happy for friends who make lovely gardens.

But don't ever
mistake
another plan
for your own.

You are the very best architect of your garden.

When you have done the work, take the credit and enjoy the praise.

Some adults try to teach
children not to brag
about what the children do.

Sometimes that lesson
can be learned too well
and people forget
that they really can take credit
for a job well done.
If something is done well,
people notice.

And very often, they will reward
the person with a compliment.

When that happens as a result
of your hard work and you have
created something worthwhile,
(like your garden) by all means,
take the credit and say
"Thank you".

That's all the

gardening advice I have.

But, you know, as I read this over,
it seems to me that these gardening
thoughts have a lot to do
with making a life.

So, maybe the ideas in this book are
really about what we all can do to
make a beautiful life.

What did you say?
You had already figured that out?

Well, you are just as smart as
I thought you were!

Made in the USA
San Bernardino, CA
24 January 2018